Nature's Smallest Gravedigger

Nature's Smallest Gravedigger

BY VICTORIA COX AND STAN APPLEBAUM

ILLUSTRATED BY DOROTHEA BARLOWE

Under the General Editorship of Vera R. Webster

GOLDEN PRESS • NEW YORK
WESTERN PUBLISHING COMPANY, INC.
RACINE, WISCONSIN

Would you believe that I can make that unfortunate mole over there disappear from the face of the earth?

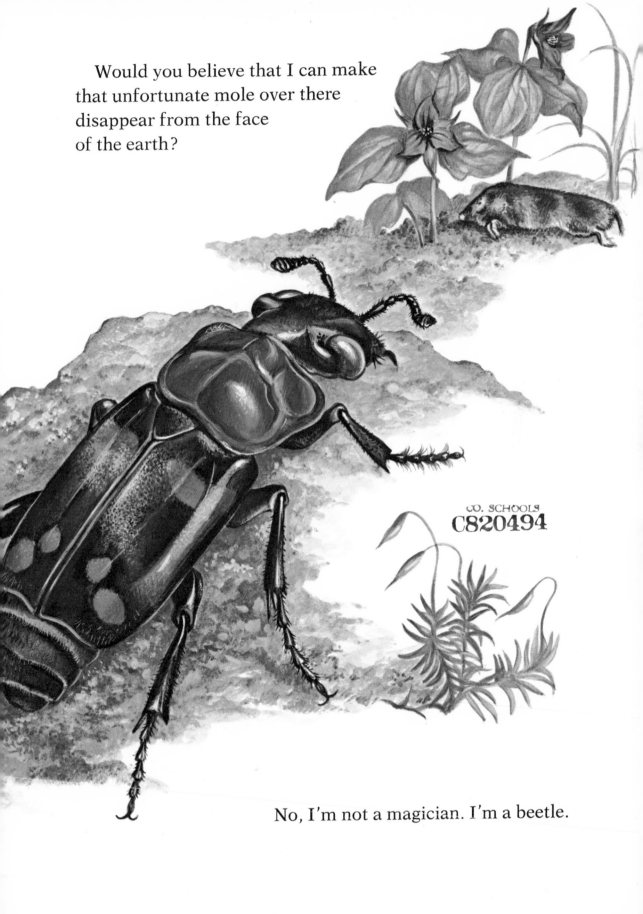

No, I'm not a magician. I'm a beetle.

But, I'm more than just an ordinary beetle. I perform a special role in Nature's Sanitation Corps. This unique clean-up corps consists of a variety of animals, birds, insects, and sea creatures that help keep land and water areas clean and healthy. They eat decaying matter before it becomes a breeding ground for disease germs.

I'm a land member of Nature's Sanitation
Corps. But, unlike most of the other land
members, I don't get rid of decaying matter by
eating it all right away.

When you look at my size and then look at the
size of this dead creature, you can probably
figure out why. I'm only about an inch long...
and a creature such as this mole is one hundred
times my size.

The mole is far too large for me to eat in just one meal. It is enough food for many meals. Therefore, after finding such a large treasure of food—why should I let it go to waste? I don't. I store it in an "underground savings bank." In other words, I quickly bury it.

By doing this, bacteria in the soil helps ripen
the flesh so that it is easier for me to eat. And
burying my treasure quickly, is the best way
of hiding it from larger creatures that might come
along and either gulp it down or walk off with it.

If the creature happens to be on soil that I can dig into, I'll perform an "on the spot" or an "instant burial." I'm commonly known as "The Burying Beetle." To be more precise, the American Burying Beetle.

However, some people refer to me as the Sexton Beetle. The word "sexton" means the person who was responsible for tolling the bell and digging graves in country churchyards.

If you find a dead creature lying on the ground, you might see a whole variety of beetles crawling around it. Some of these are probably Carrion and Rove beetles. They also help get rid of decaying organisms by eating them, but they do not bury the creature. "That's my job."

You probably need a magnifying glass to pick me out from the rest. I'm black with red spots on my wing covers and a red spot on the center of my head.

Looking very closely, you can see how nature has designed me for my special task. My legs are covered with spikes and have hooks at the ends. I use these "tools" to plow and shovel soil. I also have a pair of antennae that are covered with thousands of tiny pits especially adapted for detecting odors. You might say, it's like having thousands of tiny noses.

Under my wing covers are a pair of strong wings. They allow me to fly long distances and cover a lot of territory as I search for creatures that have died.

Unlike many other insects or beetles, my
antennae are not "tuned into" the odors of sweet
smelling flowers: they are "tuned into" the odor
of decaying organisms. These odors might smell
unpleasant to you . . . but they mean food for me.

If too many other beetles are feeding on a carcass, I might spread my wing covers and take off to find a feast for myself.

With antennae thrust out, I soar in the air until I get a whiff of something decaying. Then spiralling downward, I try to find out where the odor is coming from.

Obviously, I cannot bury something as large as a moose; but if I find a small creature (such as an insect, bird, chipmunk, mouse, frog, or lizard), I'll land nearby, fold my wings, and begin to survey the situation.

First, I examine the creature by touching it
with my forelegs and antennae. Then, rolling
over on my back, with my legs extended, I
squeeze underneath its body. Righting myself,
and using my forelegs as shovels, I start digging
in several spots to test the soil for hardness.

If the area is rocky, I might try to move the
creature. I use my hind legs like a jack to lift the
body and then push it. But, if the creature is too
large for me to move by myself, I sometimes
fly off to find help from other burying beetles.

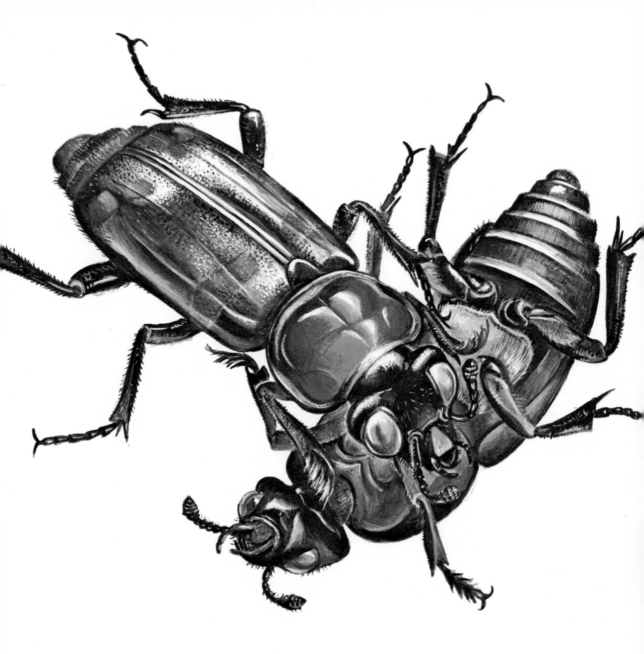

   However, more than likely, another burying
beetle has already gotten a whiff of my find and
is probably on its way. Unless the beetle is of
the opposite sex and can be my mate, I usually
end up in a "fight to the finish" to protect
my treasure.

If the beetle is of the opposite sex, we pair up and work together as a team. Once the large carcass is buried, it will provide a source of food for us as well as for our young.

Crawling underneath the dead animal, my new mate and I use our legs to loosen the soil and shovel it away.

Then we push the soil out from underneath the
carcass with our heads and bodies, leaving
tiny ditches in the soil. Slowly, gravity and the
weight of the animal cause it to sink downward
and fill these tiny openings.

The more soil we dig away... the deeper the
animal sinks.

Perhaps the most fascinating part of this whole burying process is what happens to the soil that we shovel away.

We push it into tiny piles around the outer edge of the creature. These piles are placed in such a way that with each sinking movement of the body, the soil caves inward too. The soil that was once underneath the carcass slowly becomes the soil that covers it.

We know that everything is working smoothly if we can feel the dead animal resting on our backs as we work. However, if we do not feel the animal, we usually crawl out from underneath it and try to figure out what has happened.

Quite often the dead animal might be resting on a twig. Since it is usually impossible to move the twig, the only logical solution is to chew through it.

And that's exactly what we do.

Unfortunately, with the final "chomp," the
carcass often comes crashing downward, causing
what feels like a miniature earthquake to us.
But somehow we usually manage to live through
it all and continue our work.

The gravedigging is complete when there are about two inches of soil covering the body. But we have one more task ahead of us. We need to dig tunnels leading to our underground food supply. In one of these passageways, the female burying beetle lays her eggs. We both watch the eggs carefully until they hatch, and then feed them from the decaying carcass.

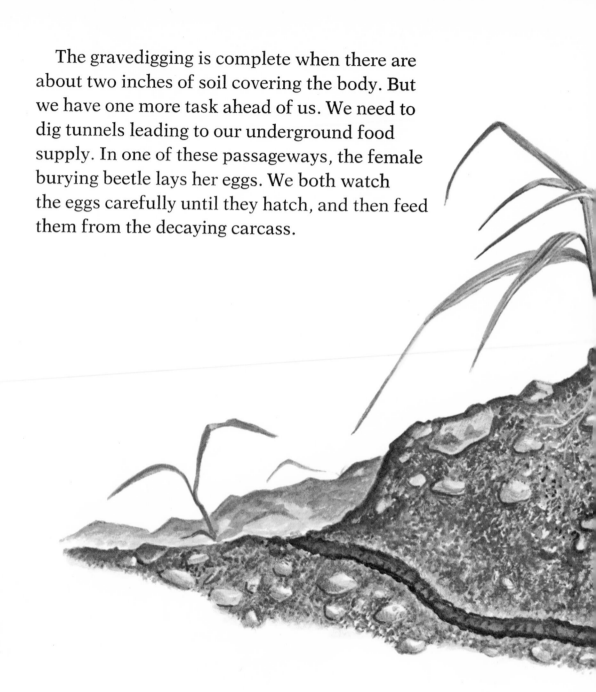

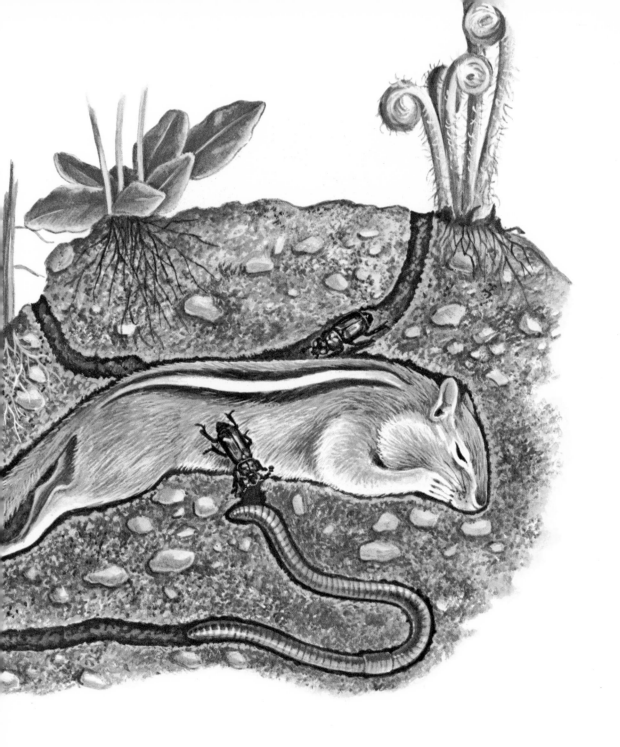

Once in a while we have to ward off unwanted
visitors who try to eat our food supplies.

When the young beetles (or larvae) are ready
to pupate (or change into the adult beetle form),
we prepare rooms for them and then leave them
on their own.

Once they emerge as adult beetles, they have to soar through the air and find their own food.
No one is around to warn them about burying a large carcass quickly.

But they soon learn why it's necessary to be an *instant* gravedigger!